Published by Red Wand Publishing

Granny Annie and the Happy Moon Cats

Printed in the U.S.A.

For permission requests, write to reesagrace.author@gmail.com

ISBN: 978-0-6483872-3-7

Written & Illustrated by Reesa Grace

This is Granny Annie. She had a dream of making people happy with her delicious warm bread.

Granny waited but no customers came.

"Will my dream ever come true?" she sighed.

Until one night, her life was about to change forever. There was a knock on the door.

When she opened the door, a strange little cat was staring at her.

"Hi Granny Annie! Nice to meet you. My mom wants to speak to you. Please follow me."

And there she met Mama Moon Cat...

"I'm the Happy Moon Cat, the bringer of happiness. And these are my children. We heard you and will help you make the world a happier place."

Granny was reluctant.

"...But isn't the world too big for me?"

Mama Moon Cat smiled. "Nothing is impossible," she said and flew back into the sky leaving all the little Moon Cats with Granny.

Bread Shop

Once inside the shop, the Moon Cats started jumping around. It was a mess! Granny Annie wasn't sure what to do.

All she had to feed them was warm bread. The cats stopped to eat. It was the most delicious bread they'd ever had!

Not so long there was another knock on the door...

A poor man was standing there.

"Hello Miss. I'm starving. Could you give me something to eat?"

Granny Annie let him in and gave him warm bread too.

"This is the most delicious bread I've ever had!" he said. The Moon Cats agreed. And Granny Annie was pleased.

When the man was full, he thanked Granny Annie and went on his way happy.

Suddenly, one Happy Moon Cat jumped right after him.

She and the Moon Cat had saved his life. Soon the man became a popular musician. He was never poor again.

And she would never know...

The man also told a crying little girl and her mother about the bread shop.

Soon they were in front of Granny Annie's shop.

"Hello! Are you still open?"

Granny Annie let them in and gave them warm bread.

"This is the most delicious bread I've ever had!" the girl said. The Moon Cats agreed. And Granny Annie was pleased.

When the girl and her mother were full, they thanked Granny Annie and went on their way happy.

Suddenly, two Happy Moon Cats jumped right after them.

Granny Annie would never know..

She and the Moon Cats had cheered them up. Soon the girl started to walk again.

And she would never know...

They met a lady who had a lot of worries and told her about the bread shop.

Soon she was in front of Granny Annie's shop.

"Hi. I just heard a lovely story about your shop."

Granny Annie let her in and gave her warm bread.

"This is the most delicious bread I've ever had!" the woman said. The Moon Cats agreed. And Granny Annie was pleased.

When the woman was full, she thanked Granny Annie and went on her way happy.

This time... not one, not two but many Happy Moon Cats jumped right after her!

Granny Annie would never know...

The woman took the Moon Cats to the old people she was taking care of.

And they started to enjoy their lives again.

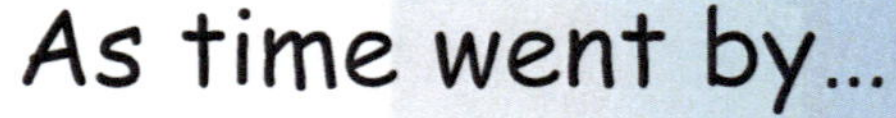

As time went by...

...people were spreading word about the bread shop and how it had improved their lives.

Soon, the once-quiet shop had become very busy!

People queued up for the most delicious bread they'd ever had.

The Moon Cats followed their people back.
Now, happiness was everywhere.

One night, Mama Moon Cat came to see Granny Annie again.

"You are smiling Granny," said the Moon Cat.

"That's because my dream has come true."

"There's so much more to do. Are you ready for it?" Mama Moon Cat asked. Granny Annie gave her a big hug.

Mama Moon Cat was right ...

...the world is never too big for us to share happiness...

About Author

Reesa Grace was born in Bangkok, the most vibrant city of Thailand. Since her childhood, she has always been passionate about Western fairy tales especially the princess stories. Her biggest dream is to share her stories to the world and now she is living it! Apart from wandering around in her own fantasy world, she enjoys spending time with two adorable cats that often interrupt her daydreaming.

She can be found online at

Facebook: www.facebook.com/reesagrace
Instagram: @reesagrace

Made in the USA
San Bernardino, CA
21 March 2019